Easy
Watercolor

An Introductory Course

Marcia Moses

Sterling Publishing Co., Inc.
New York

Easy Watercolor, An Introductory Course
is an abridgment of:
Easy Watercolor, Learn to Express Yourself
by Marcia Moses, © 2002 by Marcia Swartz Moses
ISBN 0-8069-9542-4

Library of Congress Cataloging-in-Publication Data Available

With all my heart, I dedicate this book to my mother, Marguerite Welsh Swartz, who gave me the courage to pursue my dreams. I know that you're that angel on my shoulder still protecting and guiding me. I love you; this song is for you. —M. M.

10 9 8 7 6 5 4 3 2

Published by Sterling Publishing Co., Inc.
387 Park Avenue South, New York, N.Y. 10016

© 2005 by Marcia Swartz Moses
Cover: *Magnolias*, Marcia Moses
Title page: *Hydrangeas*, Marcia Moses
Book design by Judith Stagnitto Abbate

Manufactured in China
All rights reserved
ISBN 0-7607-9553-3

For information about custom editions, special sales, premium and
corporate purchases, please contact Sterling Special Sales
Department at 800-805-5489 or specialsales@sterlingpub.com.

Contents

Finding the Right Tools & Materials

Finding just the right watercolor tools and materials for me took many years of painting and experimenting.

I can advise you about what materials are best for a beginner to work with, but personal likes and dislikes and individual artistic styles play a large part in each artist's selection. So I urge you to experiment on your own. Find out which brushes you feel comfortable painting with and what paints help you achieve the artistic results you wish. Don't think of it as a chore; think of it as playing. You'll be painting through the selection process.

PAPER

Many different types of watercolor paper are available, and each has a distinct use. The three most popular types of watercolor paper are hot-pressed (HP), cold-pressed (NOT), and rough. In the past, artists needed to "size" paper, often by soaking it briefly. Today most paper is of such quality that artists don't need to do that anymore.

- **Hot-pressed paper,** referred to as HP, is smooth, without a lot of texture.
- **Cold-pressed paper** is also called NOT, which means not hot-pressed. It isn't as smooth as hot-pressed paper and has a little texture.
- **Rough paper** is exactly what it claims to be: paper with lots of texture. It allows paint to fall into its many valleys, leaving the peaks without color.

ROUGH

HOT-PRESSED

COLD-PRESSED

ARTIST'S TIP

Always store paper in a flat position to prevent curling.

I use 140-pound Strathmore Imperial, 140-pound Strathmore Gemini, and 140-pound Arches for most of my work. All of these papers are cold-pressed. They all take a beating. Paint can be dabbed off them, rubbed off them, and scrubbed off them without much damage to the paper itself. Mistakes can be corrected. They're all very forgiving papers.

However, subtle differences in these papers can be used to achieve your artistic goals. Arches cold-pressed paper has a somewhat forgiving surface, but Strathmore Imperial is even more forgiving. Strathmore has a quality that makes it easier to lift paint from its surface and to get back to the paper's white color. If you plan poorly and inadvertently paint an area that you had intended to leave white, you can take a damp brush and lift the paint off and return to the desired lighter value.

While Strathmore Gemini is very similar in surface to Arches, it has a creamy tone. An artist preserving whites must be aware that those whites will not be as bright as when using some other papers.

Beginners also need to look for a better quality of paper than they might initially want to buy. They think, "I'm just starting out, so I'll practice on cheap paper." However, beginner "mistakes" are exactly why you should choose better-quality paper. (I feel that there are no real mistakes—just happy accidents that can be turned into new directions.) I'd suggest using at least 140-pound paper because it's going to hold up especially when you want to scrub the paint off. The only reason a beginner might want to use a rough paper is to

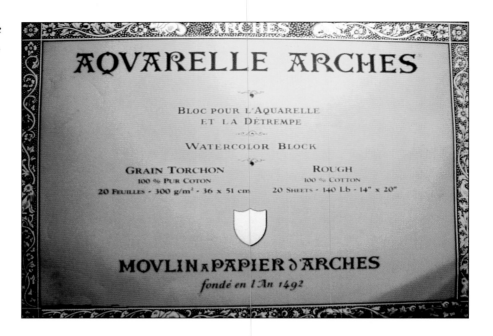

Arches Rough Paper Block
This paper has a forgiving surface.

take advantage of its skipping power. With rough paper, the brush will skip over small sections and miss certain parts of the paper, leaving a sparkling appearance.

Hot-Pressed or Cold-Pressed?

Hot-pressed paper accepts a smoother wash and can be used, for example, when painting a misty landscape. Paint soaks into the paper in a smooth, nontextured manner. Cold-pressed paper is the most versatile. You can do just about anything on it.

Paper Size

What size of paper to use is also an obvious question for the beginner. The usual advice for novices—start small—may not apply to people beginning to learn watercolor art. Granted, a beginner won't want to start with a full 22 × 30 sheet of paper. An entire blank sheet of paper can be intimidating no matter how large. But, it's not wise for a beginner to start too small, either. That's because you have the urge to stay at that size of paper and not to give yourself room to grow as an artist. Try doing a painting or two on a one-eighth sheet of paper; then quickly move up to quarter sheets and even half sheets.

Paper Pad or Block

Why not just buy a pad or a block of watercolor paper and be done with it? Well, pads and blocks can be more expensive than buying paper in packets of individual sheets. And those individual sheets can be broken down into the size of paper with which you want to work. Blocks and pads limit an artist pretty much to the size the blocks or pads are cut. However, blocks are certainly convenient, especially when painting outside, if only to carry. Blocks also eliminate the need for a backing board.

My advice: Try out a variety of paper, and decide after you paint on it what you feel most comfortable with. Do a similar painting with the same colors on a variety of papers to see how the paint reacts. In other words, play.

FINDING THE RIGHT PAINT

PAINT IS ALSO a matter of personal preference.

The most important thing to keep in mind about watercolor paint is not to consider yourself a student. At least avoid using student-grade paint. This paint is inexpensive but contains less pigment than higher grades of paint. The quality is not as good, and the artwork produced using student-grade paints will also suffer. You want to begin with the confidence that you are better than student-grade paints. If you do, you will be.

Pan-and-Cake Paints

How do you recognize student-grade paint? Those inexpensive six-color pans of paints generally are student grade. You can buy higher-quality pan-and-cake paints, and they will have the advantage of convenience. You can travel more easily with them. Pan paints also can be stored with ease. They generally come in sets, so you get many different colors. But, it's tough to do a major wash with a small pan of paint, without adding a lot of water.

Pan-and-Cake Paints
These come with a variety of colors and can be stored easily. You can buy some cakes singly, in small groups, or already in wells of convenient carrying cases.

ARTIST'S TIP

When it's not in use, cover the palette to prevent mold from forming on the paints.

Tube Paints

I recommend that you begin by filling a palette with tube paints, perhaps starting with only the three primary colors and adding a color or two at intervals over time as you become accustomed to the properties of each color. Tube colors usually are of higher quality, and frequently, they're fresher.

I've used many different brands of paint and found Holbein paints work best for me. Holbein does not use ox gall, a wetting agent, in its paint. The colors are noted for their lightfast qualities and physical permanence, both individually and in mixture. There are many qualities I really appreciate about Holbein paints, but the most important reason I use them is because it's easy to read the properties of each color. I find it helpful knowing what a color will do and how it will react in many situations.

Tube Paints
Tube paints are usually of higher quality and fresher than cake paints.

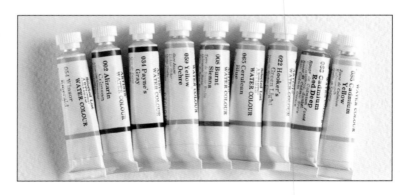

BRUSHES

PERHAPS THE MOST valuable tools you'll ever own are your brushes. It's extremely important to buy the best from the very beginning. With the right brushes, you'll benefit in your art and learning.

Kolinsky sable brushes are considered the finest brushes on the market. I own many of them. However, quality is not necessarily costly. Personally, I prefer the relatively inexpensive Holbein or Jack Richeson brushes. Unlike some artists, who believe that only a Kolinsky sable brush can do the job, I use my Holbein and Jack Richeson brushes almost exclusively. Naturally, we all have different ways of moving and seeing and need to use the tools we feel most comfortable with. Try out several different brushes and make your own choices.

It took me a while to find the right combination that works for me, but in my art, I use a few brushes consistently. These include: 1½-inch flat, 1-inch flat, ¾-inch flat, ½-inch flat, #18 round, and #4 round. The 1½-inch flat brush is great for large washes and glazes.

Brush Varieties
Brushes are an artist's most valuable tools. Choose them with care.

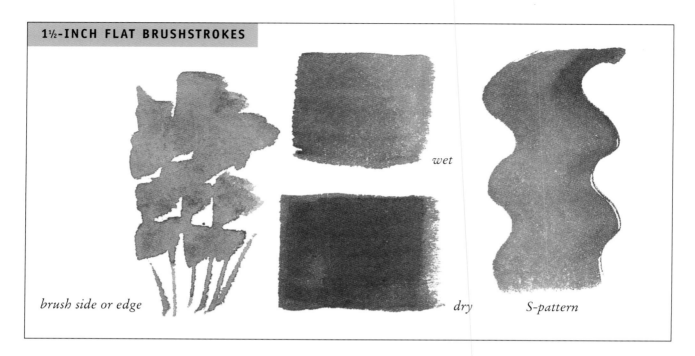

1½-INCH FLAT BRUSHSTROKES

brush side or edge

wet

dry   S-pattern

A 1½-inch brush created the vertical stroke; I used the side and the edge of the brush. The two wide strokes (in the center) were made with a wet brush (top) and dry brush (bottom). Moving the brush in an S-pattern created the stroke on the right.

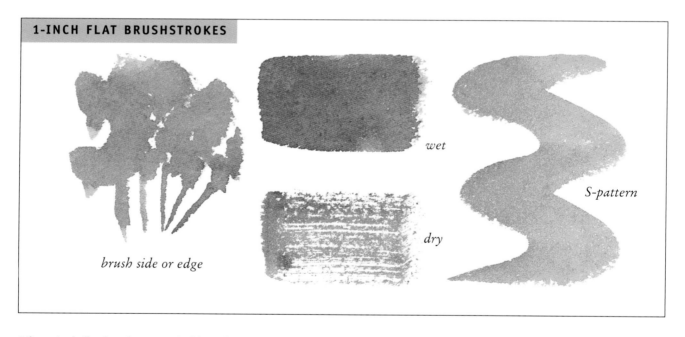

1-INCH FLAT BRUSHSTROKES

brush side or edge

wet

dry

S-pattern

The 1-inch flat brush creates bold strokes; it's also good for washes or glazes. These brushes come in various brands and hair types. Many artists claim Kolinsky sable is the best. Certainly, it is the most expensive. If a brush creates the result you're working for, then that brush is for you, regardless of cost. Here are some strokes you can achieve with a 1-inch flat brush on 140-pound Arches paper.

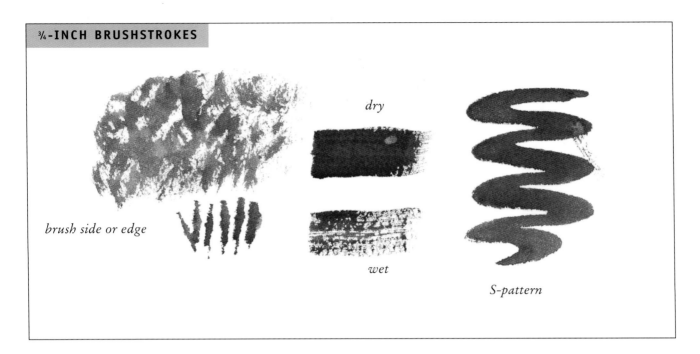

¾-INCH BRUSHSTROKES

dry

brush side or edge

wet

S-pattern

These strokes were made with a 1-inch flat brush on 140-pound Arches paper. The 1-inch flat brush works in much the same way as the 1-inch, although it's smaller and will make narrower strokes.

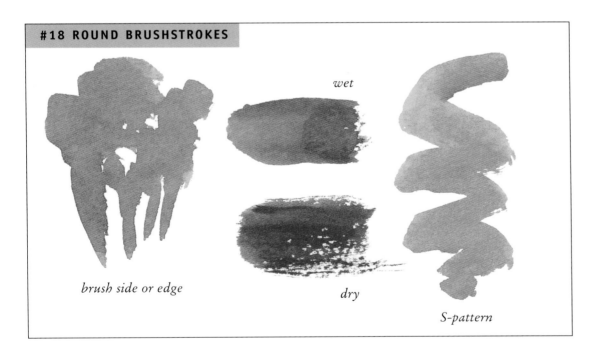

#18 ROUND BRUSHSTROKES

wet

brush side or edge

dry

S-pattern

These strokes were made with a #18 round brush on 140-pound Arches paper. It makes much smoother strokes than a flat brush with softer edges. It can be used for larger details.

½-INCH FLAT BRUSHSTROKES

brush side or edge

wet

dry

S-pattern

Here are examples of strokes made by a ½-inch flat brush on 140-pound Arches paper. The ½-inch flat brush is great for getting into and around edges of shapes in paintings.

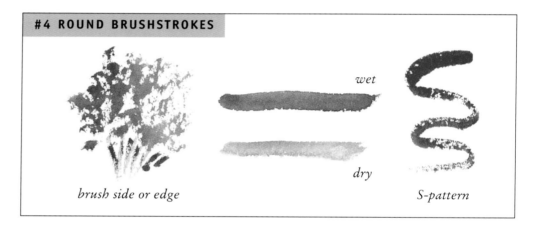

#4 ROUND BRUSHSTROKES

wet

dry

brush side or edge

S-pattern

These strokes were made with a #4 round brush on 140-pound Strathmore Imperial paper. The #4 round is used for fine detail, drawing lines, and lettering.

PALETTES

I USE TWO TYPES of palette: a butcher's tray and the Robert E. Wood palette. However, many useful palettes are available in the market. Find one that suits you.

When I'm throwing paint, I use a butcher's tray. It's also useful for spattering, or any other technique that frees you to mix paint in a less controlled way. The palette's smooth enamel finish allows the paint to run together to form beautiful and surprising colors. Some-

Butcher's Tray or Palette

Robert E. Wood Palette

times I transfer luminous patterns from the butcher's tray onto watercolor paper by laying the paper on top of it so that the paper absorbs the pretty colors and patterns. This creates a wonderful background; it also helps you avoid wasting paint.

However, the palette I prefer and use most is the Robert E. Wood, named after the artist who developed it. This very efficient palette has large paint wells and a generous divided mixing space that allows you to mix two different washes at one time.

It allows you more control over your colors. The wells are deep and hold a lot of paint. On the side of the palette, there's space to write the names of colors. You can even store the palette with paint left in the wells. The cover of the palette has four mixing wells, so you can mix as many as six colors at once.

PAINTING SUPPORTS

To PREVENT WATERCOLOR paper from buckling, you'll need to support it. The support needs to be comfortably positioned for your work. Most artists use tape or bulldog clips to attach paper to a wooden board, gator board, or Plexiglas. The support prevents the paper from developing wrinkles when you apply water, and it provides a stable surface for painting. If you then place the board or Plexiglas support on an easel or drafting table, you'll be able to position the paper at an angle that's comfortable for painting.

I use my painting table more often than my easel, although there are many reasons to use an easel. You may like to stand when you paint; I do. I feel in control in this position. I do have a French easel that I use when on location, and that works out well for me because of the flat position the easel allows. Most of the time when I paint *en plein air* (outside), I just prop my board on something and assume a comfortable position.

Whatever painting support you use, it's important to find a home for it. When I began painting, I used the kitchen table. However, for many years I was hesitant to paint because it took so much work to set up. Find a space of your own that you can go to for painting. You don't want to be deterred by the work it would take to get started or by the many possible distractions of life's everyday events. I love the freedom my studio provides. Designate a space for your painting activities that you can use regularly, and keep supplies ready.

OTHER SUPPLIES

KEEP A COLOR WHEEL with your painting supplies for reference. You'll find many color wheels on the market. The Color Wheel Company makes a great pocket color guide with an abundance of information that supplements the traditional color wheel.

Use masking fluid to preserve whites. I favor Incredible White Mask liquid frisket. Before I learned how best to apply this mask, I ruined too many brushes to count. Now I use the same brush every time I apply a mask. Lather the brush with an unadultered soap, like Ivory soap. The soap protects the brush from becoming gummy as long as you soap it between each stroke. Then brush the mask on paper area you want to stay white or unpainted until later. Another way to preserve whites is to use masking tape. Of course, you may not be able to achieve some of the same subtlety you can with masking fluid.

Watercolor artists also need drawing materials. Begin each painting with a value sketch and a design sketch. Find a sketchbook you're comfortable with and some drawing pencils. I favor using a #2B or #3B pencil for sketching because these pencils contain a soft lead that, when combined with a soft touch, will leave a light impression. A soft gum eraser or a kneaded eraser will not damage the paper surface of sketchbook or watercolor paper.

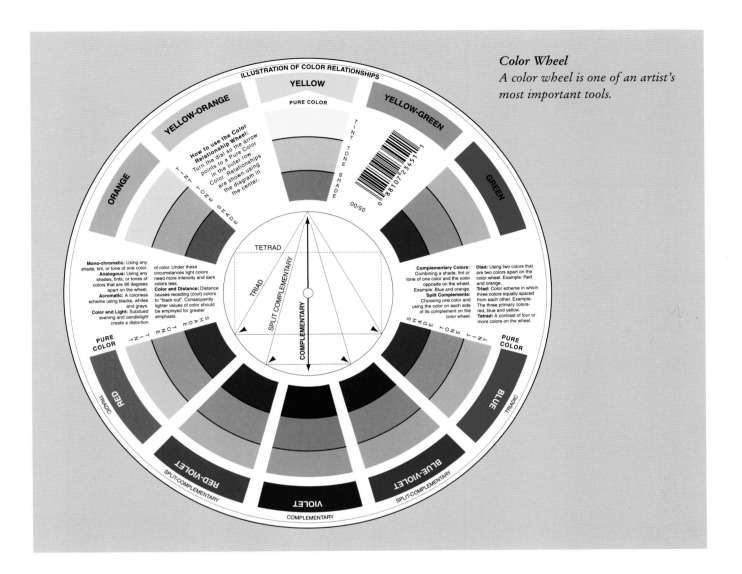

Household Tools

A surprising number of household items can do double duty as artist's tools. Spatter or scrub out paint with old toothbrushes. Move paint around the painting with a spray bottle or atomizer filled with water or alcohol. Clean brushes or lift paint to create shapes, like clouds, with tissue and paper towels. Create texture on a wet paint surface with plastic wrap and wax paper. Shift paint around with a razor blade. Just use your imagination to discover the variety of objects around the house that you'll want to add to your painter's toolbox.

Shaping
Composition & Design

THE WATERCOLOR ARTIST creates a three-dimensional illusion on a two-dimensional piece of paper. It is just so long and so wide. Within this area the artist creates a feeling of distance as infinite as the sky. At the same time, some things must appear realistically close—so near that the viewer believes he can reach out and feel both the roughness of a rock and the softness of a flower petal.

Composition refers to the total content of a work of art, and *design* refers to the arrangement of elements of the work.

ABOUT SPACE

SPACE EXISTS IN a painting only as an illusion, but it gives life to the visual design. Flowers, lighthouses, and other forms have substance, so the space they occupy in the picture is sometimes known as *occupied space.* The area around them is unoccupied space, or *negative space.* Hold your hand at arm's length and extend your fingers. The fingers represent occupied space (positive space). The area between the fingers is unoccupied space (negative space).

Even if you stretch your fingers out so that the space between them seems almost equal, there's still a difference. Note the space between the thumb and forefinger and between the little finger and the ring finger. Now, move two of the fingers closer together. Notice how the change in the space changes the entire design.

Because the only whites we have in watercolor are the paper and the water, we more often paint in the negative or unoccupied space behind a form that must be light or dark to show its shape.

To understand negative space, think about space that an object occupies. Look behind it to see what does not exist; this is negative space. Negative space brings to life the object that you're trying to make stand out. Understanding positive and negative space is one of the most important concepts in design. It applies to all art media, including watercolor.

LIGHT & DARK COLORS

LIGHT NEXT TO dark creates tension. Dark will push objects back. Light will make objects come forward.

These are the facts of life in art. They're not my ideas, but what you or I choose to do with them are our own personal interpretation(s). The masters gave us so many tools and concepts, that being an artist is easier today than in past centuries. These tools and concepts help our own personal creativity to soar.

If you apply the seven basic elements of design, you'll be successful. It's important to allow yourself to make mistakes, forgive yourself, and move on. This is all part of the learning process. We learn by taking artistic and intellectual risks.

ARTIST'S TIP

To create unity, use at least three design elements in each painting.

Yesterday
Marcia Moses and
Wanda Montgomery
16 × 20 inches

The Seven Elements of Design

Design exists in everything around us, from the simplest flower to the most complex human structure. To design is to have purpose.

Designing in art means deliberate planning and arranging elements in a way that creates a unified effect. When used together, all design elements help create unity in a painting. The seven elements of design—shape, size, line, texture, value, color, and form—are the building blocks of an artwork.

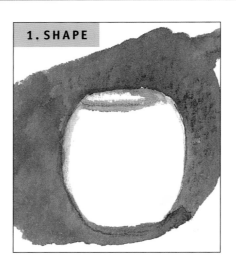

1. SHAPE

Any object with height and width has a shape. A positive shape automatically creates a negative shape.

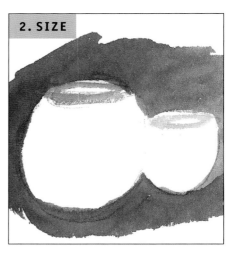

2. SIZE

Size is very simply the relationship of the area occupied by one shape to that area occupied by another shape.

6. COLOR

Watercolors are basically pigments ground in water and bound with gum. Color is what that pigment is: red, yellow, blue, orange, green, violet, etc.

7. FORM

Form, the surface characteristics of an object, describes an object's three-dimensional qualities, such as its roundness or volume. The object's shape suggests the form, but its true nature is revealed through the variations of light and shadow. Sometimes direction replaces form as a design element.

DESIGN ELEMENTS COMBINED

When you combine all seven elements, the painting can become busy. It's better to use just three or four of these elements, like the painting on page 19 (bottom). This painting combines the elements of shape, color, form, and size.

3. LINE

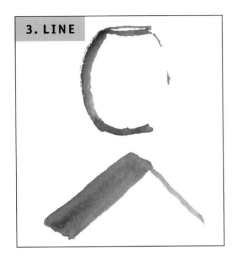

There are two ways to describe line: the marks made with a pen, pencil, or brush, or the edge created when two lines meet.

4. TEXTURE

Texture is the surface condition of a shape: rough or smooth with a hard or soft edge. Texture can be physical and tactile, or it can be merely a visual illusion.

5. VALUE

The value of a hue is determined by its intensity. A value range from 0 to 10 has 10 as void of color and 0 as the full color. (Some value scales may reverse that and give 10 as full color and 0 as void of color.)

COMBINED ELEMENTS

METRIC EQUIVALENTS

0.63 cm = ¼ inch	
1.25 cm = ½ inch	
2.54 cm = 1 inch	
3.8 cm = 1½ inches	
5 cm = 2 inches	
10 cm = 4 inches	
20 cm = 8 inches	
25 cm = 10 inches	
30 cm = 12 inches = 1 foot	
1 meter = 39 inches	
1 ounce = 28 grams	
1 pound = 448 grams	

Standard 140-pound watercolor paper is usually 500 sheets (a ream), each measuring one square meter.

Grammage: 525 grams/square meter

Unity Placement of design elements in relation to one another to create a psychologically and aesthetically pleasing whole. All design elements in a painting play off or interact with one another.

Harmony The visually satisfying effect of combining similar related design elements or objects in a painting, such as colors adjacent to each other on the color wheel, or similar shapes or textures.

Balance Avoiding a lopsided appearance in a painting; creating equilibrium. Directional lines at different angles, distribution and intensity of color, and proportionate areas allotted to significant and secondary parts of the composition contribute to the painting's balance.

Rhythm In a work of art, variety and repetition of design elements create rhythm.

Contrast The juxtaposition of dissimilar elements, such as color, tone, or emotion, in a work of art. The artist can play light against dark, soft against hard, or warm against cool. Locate the major contrast in a painting at the center of interest.

Dominance Resolving conflicting ideas by making one idea or element, such as color or direction, more important than other competing ones. Usually, one area of a painting is dominant. The painting's center of interest or focal point dominates the rest of the painting.

Gradation This creates a three-dimensional effect with different tones or grades of color from dark to light or warm to cool. The decreasing or increasing strength of shades, tints, or values of color create gradation. Gradation helps produce interest, define areas in a painting, and provide smooth transitions.

DISCOVERING HOT SPOTS

THE ELEMENTS AND principles of design used together in an orderly fashion make up the composition of a painting. Using the simple grid will allow you to create an organized work of art.

Here's a procedure for creating a simple grid: **(1)** In every rectangle there are two squares. The way to find the two squares is to measure the shortest side of the paper and then measure in that distance from the edge of the long side. For example, if you are working on an 11×15-inch piece of paper, your shortest side is 11 inches. So 11 inches would be the distance you would measure into the rectangle from the corner of its long side. Draw a line from the top to the bottom of the paper. Measure the same distance from the other side, and draw another vertical line. (2) There also are two diagonals in every rectangle. Draw a line from the top right to the bottom left corner, and another from the top left to the bottom right corner. These diagonal lines will meet in the middle. This establishes the center of the paper. (3) Then draw two horizontal lines that intersect both the vertical and diagonal lines. (4) Find the resulting hot spots, where you need to place the painting's center of interest.

Drawing a Grid for Finding Hot Spots

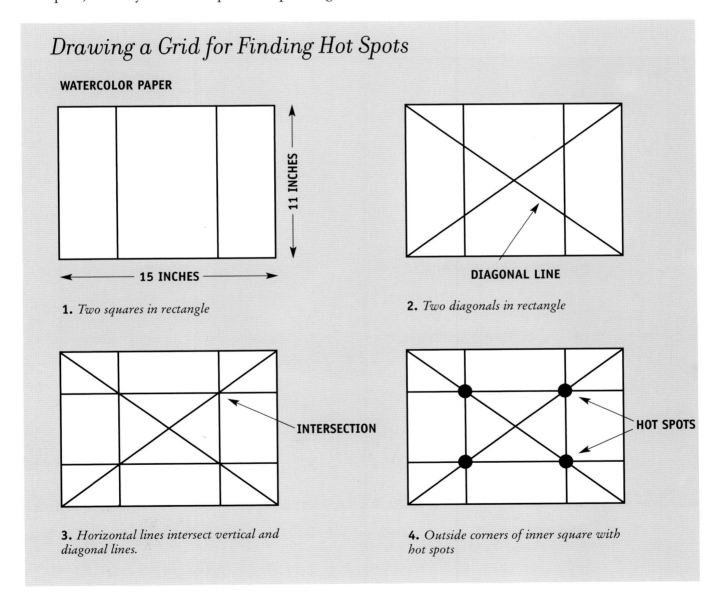

WATERCOLOR PAPER

11 INCHES

◄——— 15 INCHES ———►

1. *Two squares in rectangle*

DIAGONAL LINE

2. *Two diagonals in rectangle*

INTERSECTION

3. *Horizontal lines intersect vertical and diagonal lines.*

HOT SPOTS

4. *Outside corners of inner square with hot spots*

The viewer's eye naturally goes to the hot spots, the points where the vertical and diagonal lines meet at the corners of an inner square. (Painters and photographers also call this the "rule of thirds.") If an artist places important shapes or the center of interest in any of these four areas, the viewer's eyes will be led into the painting at the spot the artist desires. It is most common to bring a viewer into a painting from the lower left corner, leading him up the diagonal to the hot spot, then allowing less important shapes to guide him through the rest of the work of art.

If you have your center of interest in the center of the paper, your viewer is going to be led directly to that area and stop, with nowhere else to go. Look for the hot spots, and use them to improve your *design,* the arrangement of elements in your artwork.

Winter Solstice
Marcia Moses, 11 × 14 inches

The house in this watercolor is located in one of the painting's hot spots.

LEARNING TO SEE

In order to increase your visual awareness, you need to learn how to see as an artist. How do we see things differently than we do now? We do that by becoming more aware of what it is that we're looking at.

To do that, first look at an object. Let's try a tree. Now squint your eyes. Squinting your eyes creates a frame that helps you more clearly see the darks and the lights of objects.

Now look behind the lighter objects. What do you see? Dark shapes? This is called negative space.

Squint again. What else do you see? Do you see some shapes that are lighter than others or darker than others? Lighter objects will appear to come forward and darker objects will recede.

The difference between the lightest and darkest of the objects is the difference in what is called *value.*

However, there are more values than just light and dark. The shadowed side of the tree is going to be darker than the lighted side of the tree, but not as dark as the tree's background. This in-between dark and light is called a middle value.

Begin to look at everything as values: darks, lights, and middle values.

It's amazing all that you can see when you begin to see as an artist does.

"Your vision will become clear Only when you look into your own heart.
He who looks outside dreams.
He who looks inside Awakes."

—MARC CHAGALL (1887–1985)

Tree
Marcia Moses, 4 × 5 inches

Photo of Annasquam Light in Gloucester, Massachusetts

Seize the Moment

Along with your sketchbook, make a camera your close companion. We stumble upon beauty when we least expect it. We never know when a sunset will offer lively colors that hit water so perfectly they almost seem to dance. If you have your camera, you can capture that image in a picture, and use that photo at a later date to reproduce the image on paper or canvas.

Being an artist today is so much easier than it was in the past. We are so fortunate to be able to capture moments of beauty on film. Claude Monet painted water lilies many times to reproduce in a painting what he saw as the perfect light. Imagine what a visual memory he must have had. The camera can remember what we forget.

I always carry my camera when I am painting *en plein air.* The light can change so rapidly that the very essence of what I am looking at can disappear in an instant. Seize the moment with a camera.

DRAWING

BEING ABLE TO draw, not just to paint, is important to an artist.

If you sketch your subject before painting it, you'll not only create an outline for your artwork, but you'll also get to know each object inside and out. Whenever you draw an object, say for example an apple, you not only have to draw the front part of the apple. You must create the illusion that the apple has a back side without actually showing that side of it. Viewers must see the apple's curvature and believe that it isn't flat. Drawing each object will help you give them three dimensions.

When you begin drawing an object, think of it as a shape and forget about detail. When you're painting a lighthouse, think of the bottom of the lighthouse as a cylinder, the top as an ellipse, and the roof as a triangle. If you simplify the object into such basic shapes, it will be easier to draw.

Once you've established all the basic shapes, you'll have what is called a *value sketch.* Determine what are the lightest parts of the object and what are its darkest darks.

Sketch of Annasquam Light

Annasquam Light
Marcia Moses, 11 × 14 inches

Squinting to See

This little exercise will help you draw what you see with more depth, shape, and accuracy, thereby improving the illusion.

1. Look at a tree.
2. Squint your eyes to create a frame for the image.
3. Look at the values in the image and behind the image; see the darks and the lights.
4. What shapes do you see within the tree?
5. What shapes make up the negative space behind the tree?
6. Begin to draw the tree's overall shape (the positive space). When your drawing takes on the shape, texture, and depth of what you're seeing, put down your pencil and pick up your brush.

Photo of Lanterns

Mystic Lanterns
Marcia Moses, 22 × 30 inches

READ ABOUT IT

A number of excellent books deal with drawing and how to reproduce what you see. Here are my favorites:

Stan Smith, *Step-by-Step Drawing* (Sterling, 1994)

Michael J. Gelb, *How to Think Like Leonardo da Vinci* (Delacorte Press, 1998)

Betty Edwards, *Drawing on the Right Side of Your Brain* (Tarcher/Putnam, 1979)

Color Wheel with Gray Scale
A pocket color wheel, like that shown here, usually includes a gray scale with values ranging from 1 to 10.

Value is the lightness or darkness of a color. I have a value scale that measures values from 1 to 10. On this scale, 10 is the lightest. (If you wish, you could have 10 as the darkest and 1 as the lightest.) Here we will be working with the lightest or white of your paper as 10 and the darkest value as 1.

Consider using a common gray scale. Practice using this scale to produce sketches that show varying shapes. But use only two, three, or four values. As you add more values, notice how your drawings take on more depth. However, adding too many values can make a drawing too busy, and the artist could get confused. Less is more.

To make the gray scale work for you, let's consider an apple. Sketch and draw an apple to produce the shape and give the shape dimension. Here is a five-value sketch that shows its darks and lights.

Gray Scale
This gray scale has ten gradated steps from 10% off-white (1) to black (10). Compare this scale with your color to determine its specific intensity. Using colors of the same value provide the best visual results.

SIMPLIFYING
THE VALUE SCALE

I'VE RECENTLY begun to use a simplified value scale. This simplified scale makes understanding and using values less complicated.

When a painting has too many colors, it becomes very confusing for the viewer. The use of too many values has the same effect. In order to give a painting a clean appearance, we can reduce the ten values to three or five.

When we paint, we are telling a story. If that story has too much information, the "reader" will lose interest. By simplifying the painting process, we hold the viewer's interest. Again, less is more.

Simplified Value Scale

Creating a Simplified Value Scale

To create a simplified value scale, begin by mixing a large amount of cobalt blue on a palette in a ratio of one part water to five parts paint.

Use a small piece of watercolor paper 3 × 12 inches and draw a box on it that's 2 × 10 inches. Now divide this into five 2-inch spaces. These boxes will contain your five values.

Gradated Washes

**FIRST WASH
TWO-VALUE SCALE**

Begin by skipping the first box. This will be your white value. Then paint a wash over the next four boxes. Let the paint dry. Or dry it with a hair dryer; it's faster. With the paper's white and the first wash, you have a two-value scale.

TWO WASHES
THREE-VALUE SCALE

Now paint a second wash of the same paint mixture, but begin at the third box, covering the three boxes painted with the first wash. Dry this second wash.

THREE WASHES
FOUR-VALUE SCALE

Put a third layer of paint on the fifth and sixth boxes.

FOUR WASHES
FIVE-VALUE SCALE

Cover the fifth box with a fourth, final wash.

The result of the four washes is that each box has a different value. Now you have a simplified five-value scale that you can use for any painting. You could simplify this scale even further by reducing it to three values, but the five-value scale seems to work most effectively.

ARTIST'S TIP

A value scale is a very useful tool. Keep one handy whenever you paint.

HOW TO BEGIN

WHEN BEGINNING a painting, it's helpful to follow a routine to organize your thoughts. First choose your subject. Then figure out what shapes you want to use. Sketch the shapes. Decide where the lightest and darkest shapes are on your subject, breaking your subject down into five values.

Applying Values

Here's how to create a painted value sketch by adding values one by one.

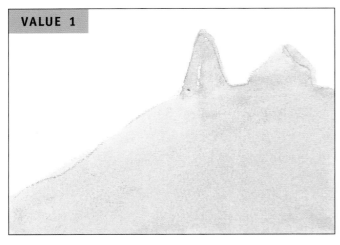

VALUE 1

First value with light wash.
In this painting the first value is applied with a light wash over the lighthouse and shapes of rocks. There are three basic shapes in the composition. The sky and rocks are the largest shape, and the lighthouse is the smallest shape.

VALUE 2

Value change with paint on rocks.
Next, apply the paint to the large rocks' shape. You can now see the value change.

VALUE 3

Three established values.

VALUE 4

Detail added to create value sketch with paint.
Begin to put another layer of the same color on top of the largest shape, the rocks. Do some negative painting, and form some smaller shapes inside the larger one. (See negative space on p. 16 and negative painting on p. 52.)

Up There
Marcia Moses, 22 × 30 inches

THE FINISHED PAINTING

I began my painting with the value sketch and then converted the value into color.

I used an aureolin yellow wash over the lighthouse and rock shapes then, while the painting still was wet, I dropped in some rose madder and let it spread on the rocks. I put a wash of ultramarine blue over the sky area. Then I dried everything and darkened the water shape with another ultramarine wash. With a third wash on the water, I skipped over a few lighter areas to show the sky's reflections in the water. After a little detailing, I was done.

Working with Color

THE STUDY OF COLOR is fascinating and vast, and some books deal with color exclusively. It is good for beginners to learn standard color terminology, color theory, and principles of color mixing. We will simply cover the basics here. Many artists have developed a fine sense of color and how to use it. However, not all artists are good colorists. If you are keen on what color can do, study it more.

THE PROPERTIES OF COLOR

HUE *an object's "local" or true color.*

The color you perceive when you look closely at an object is its *local color.* For example, green is the local color of a blade of grass in spring.

But, a green can appear quite bluish when seen from a long distance because of atmospheric effects. This is called *atmospheric color.*

Local color can also be affected by colors reflected from surrounding objects. A green apple in your still life may have hints of red in it from a neighboring red jug. The green blade of grass may have a blue-green tint as it catches the blue of the sky.

VALUE *the degree of lightness or darkness of a particular hue.*

I may look at a piece of wood and call it brown, but there are shadows on parts of the wood that make those areas darker brown. Those two shades are the same color, but different values.

Local Color of Grass

INTENSITY *a color's strength or weakness, brilliance or dullness.*

A barn can be red. But the sun shining on a part of the barn can make that area more brilliant red. And, in the same respect, a shadow on another part of the same barn can create a dull red in that area.

BASIC COLOR THEORY

A COLOR WHEEL shows us the twelve basic colors, which derive from (and include) the three primary colors. The three primary colors can be mixed to obtain the three secondary colors, which can be mixed with the primary colors to create the six tertiary colors.

Primary colors are red, yellow, and blue. You cannot create these colors by mixing other colors.

Secondary colors are orange, green, and violet. To create these colors, mix two adjacent primary colors. For example, red plus yellow makes orange, blue plus yellow makes green, and red plus blue makes violet.

Tertiary colors are yellow-orange, red-orange, yellow-green, blue-green, blue-violet, and red-violet. To produce these colors, mix a primary color with a secondary color.

Complementary colors lie directly opposite each other on the color wheel. For example, red is the complement of green, and orange is the complement of blue. If you combine a pair of complements, you can neutralize the colors and produce some very nice grays. It is often better to allow one of the colors to slightly dominate the mix to ensure that the gray is not too dull and lifeless.

Primary Colors

Secondary Colors

Transparent & Opaque Paints

If a paint color is transparent, you can see through it; it's like plastic wrap. If opaque, you can't see through the color; it's more like a brown paper bag.

Telling the Difference

Knowing when a paint color is transparent or opaque is extremely important, especially if you are glazing. You glaze one color over another in order to make the color look luminous. In order to get that luminosity in a color, you need to use transparent colors so that the other colors will show through.

For example, if you lay down a transparent yellow and dry it, and then add a layer of transparent red on top of the yellow, you'll be able to see the yellow through the red.

Here's a simple test to find out whether a color is transparent or opaque. Draw a line with a black permanent felt-tip marker. Now paint over the black line. If the line easily shows through, the color is transparent. If it doesn't, the color is opaque.

Opaque Colors

CADMIUM YELLOW-ORANGE

YELLOW OCHRE

PERMANENT YELLOW-ORANGE

CERULEAN BLUE (SEMI-TRANSPARENT)

LILAC

CADMIUM RED DEEP

CADMIUM RED-ORANGE

VERMILION

SHELL PINK

Transparent Colors

BURNT UMBER

GAMBOGE NOVA

AUREOLIN YELLOW

CADMIUM YELLOW LIGHT

HOOKER'S GREEN

ULTRAMARINE DEEP

ROYAL BLUE

COBALT BLUE

MARINE BLUE

PERMANENT ALIZARIN

LIGHT RED

OPERA

ROSE MADDER

PALE TINTS

DON'T BE TEMPTED to use white paint to achieve pale colors. In pure watercolor work, pale tints of any color are created with the help of the white of the paper and lots of water. For example, if you want a very pale blue, dilute one of your blues with plenty of water, and test the mix on a scrap of paper until you get just the pale tint you're seeking.

THE LIMITED PALETTE

THE ADVANTAGE OF using a limited palette is that it provides unity. With just the three primary colors—a red, a yellow, and a blue—you can produce a full range of secondary and tertiary colors. Your painting will naturally have a good sense of unity because all the colors you mix will contain some or all of those primary colors.

Guiding Light
Marcia Moses, 22×30 inches

Using a limited palette to create unity.

Many beautiful paintings have been created with limited palettes. You can create a high-key painting, such as "Guiding Light," that exhibits light and airy colors, by using just diluted tints of aureolin yellow, rose madder, and cobalt blue. Strong shades of dark colors, however, also are possible with this triad, if you use darker values. Mixing the colors with less water will create a low-key and rather heavy and moody painting, such as "Southwestern Vessels."

Less water creates a heavy and moody look.

Southwestern Vessels
Mary Nieto, 15 × 22 inches

COLOR TEMPERATURE

TO UNDERSTAND COLOR temperature, think of the dashboard control of a car's heater and air conditioner. Push the lever toward red to get heat. Push it toward blue to get cool air.

Actually, red is not the warmest color, and blue is not the coolest color. Viewed alone, the warmest is yellow and the coolest is black. Their relationship with each other is more important to the artist than their position on a color wheel.

The temperature of a color determines how it relates to other colors in a painting. For example, if a warm color, such as red, is placed beside a cool color, such as blue, the warm color seems to come forward and the cool color seems to recede. This is important when establishing an object's three-dimensional form or when creating the illusion of distance.

I've constructed a warm-to-cool color chart to illustrate the relative temperature of various colors. I've placed warm colors on top and cool colors on the bottom. As you'll see, some colors cannot be

Color Temperature Chart

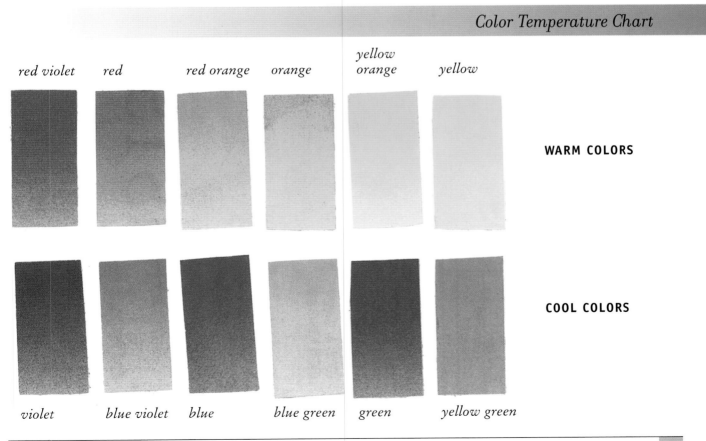

red violet   red   red orange   orange   yellow orange   yellow

WARM COLORS

COOL COLORS

violet   blue violet   blue   blue green   green   yellow green

Light warm color recedes on medium warm background.

Light warm color comes forward on medium cool background.

Light cool color comes forward on warm background.

Light cool color recedes on medium cool background.

categorized as completely warm or cool. To create this chart, I cut a color wheel in half and flattened it out. As the colors are found on a wheel, violet is beside red violet and yellow is beside yellow green. Violet, red violet, and yellow green all have qualities of both warm and cool colors.

Temperature is relative to its surroundings. In other words, warm colors recede on a warm background, and cool colors come forward on a cool background. It sounds confusing, but you can do a simple test with the colors you're using.

To demonstrate, I've created both warm and cool color background boxes. A yellow circle in the middle of a warm yellow background recedes, but a yellow dot on a cool violet background appears to come forward. A light cool blue placed on a light warm red appears to come forward, but the light cool blue placed on a medium cool blue-green will appear to recede.

Push-Pull of Warm & Cool Colors

This interaction of cool and warm colors in art is called the "push-pull" concept. If you have a cool dark color and you put a warm light color beside it, the dark color will push back. If you then place another warm color on the other side of the dark color, the light color will pull forward. This creates a three-dimensional quality in a painting, or movement.

For example, using colors that push and pull can move the eye toward and around an object, such as a lighthouse, in a painting. The cylinder shape of a lighthouse will remain flat until you use lights and darks around it to create dimension. In "Dyce Island Light" (p. 39), in order to make the lighthouse look believable, I added cool, dark shapes—shadows and trees—to allow the eye to "see" that it was a cylinder. The darks pull the eye toward the back of the lighthouse. Additional darks define the shape of the shelf at the base of the light atop the lighthouse.

I added the dark color on the roof of an adjacent building to push the house behind it into the background.

The series of warm and cool colors to the right in the foreground of the painting helps draw the viewer's eye back toward the structures that are bigger and more important shapes. The narrower series of warm and cool colors to the left in the foreground draws the eye up the diagonal, specifically to the lighthouse shape, the painting's center of interest.

Every color has a "bias" toward another color; we can call this an undertone. As we discussed when talking about warm and cool colors, a warm color, such as alizarin crimson, has a bias toward blue, or simply a blue undertone, that gives it cool tendencies. This can be a positive feature in your painting if the alizarin is mixed with a blue that also is cool, such as cobalt, if the goal is to create violet. If the blue maintains a yellow undertone, such as cerulean blue, you would create a grayed or muddy violet.

ARTIST'S TIP

To make an object stand out, use its complementary color next to it.

Muddiness

Muddiness is caused by the influence of all three primary colors on the mixture. Any time you mix all three primaries in equal parts, unless they all have the same undertone (say, yellow), you'll get muddiness. If you mixed alizarin crimson with cerulean blue that has a yellow undertone, you'd get a muddy violet.

Fresh Lilacs
Marcia Moses, 22 × 30 inches

Color Undertone or Bias

The example to the right is a mixture of aureolin yellow, alizarin crimson, and cobalt blue. You have a yellow that's blue-biased, a red that's blue-biased, and a blue that's red-biased.

We usually say the yellow has a blue undertone, the red a blue undertone, and the blue a red undertone. The result is violet.

Here are some examples of frequently used colors and their undertones or biases:

- **ALIZARIN CRIMSON (RED)**—*blue undertone*
- **COBALT BLUE**—*red undertone*
- **CERULEAN BLUE**—*yellow undertone*
- **ROSE MADDER (RED)**—*blue undertone*
- **AUREOLIN YELLOW**—*blue undertone*
- **ULTRAMARINE BLUE**—*red undertone*
- **CADMIUM YELLOW**—*red undertone*
- **CADMIUM RED**—*yellow undertone*
- **LEMON YELLOW**—*blue undertone*

Rose madder + cobalt blue → violet

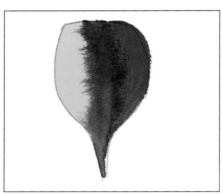

Aureolin + ultramarine blue → green

Alizarin crimson + ultramarine blue → violet

Aureolin + cobalt blue → green

Aureolin + rose madder + cobalt blue → green

Cadmium yellow light + marine blue → green

Here are some fun mixtures of colors that work well together. Try mixing your own colors to find out what you get. Make note cards with the mixtures on them for future reference. Here we use various combinations of easily available watercolors, rose madder, aureolin, cobalt blue, cadmium yellow light, marine blue, and alizarin crimson.

ARTIST'S TIP

Be aware of each color's properties and how each will react with other colors and the paper.

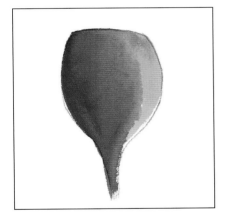

Rose madder + aureolin → orange

Aureolin + cobalt blue → green

Cadmium yellow light + marine blue → dark green

Rose madder + aureolin + cobalt blue → blue-green

Aureolin + cobalt blue + alizarin crimson → gray-green

Cadmium yellow light + marine blue + rose madder → dark gray-green

COLOR SCHEMES

Every composition should have a color scheme so that you'll have harmony in your painting. There are several different color schemes—triad, complementary, analogous, and monochromatic, among others.

A **triad color scheme** allows one choice from each of the red, yellow, and blue color families.

A **complementary color scheme** uses two colors opposite each other on the color wheel.

An **analogous color scheme** uses any three adjacent primary, secondary, or tertiary colors.

A **monochromatic color scheme** uses one color in various values.

Triad Scheme

Complementary Scheme

Analogous Scheme

Monochromatic Scheme

MIXING GRAYS

To add contrast to a composition, you need to have some darker values. So, in order to create a darker value than you can get from a single color, you need to mix two colors and often to add a third color. This will darken, or gray, the color scheme in that area.

You can mix grays in triad, complementary, analogous, monochromatic, and split-complementary color schemes as follows:

Triad Mix semi-neutrals, or grays, by using two of the colors in the triad with the third added to gray the two colors.

Complementary These colors automatically gray each other when mixed.

Triad of Grays or Semi-Neutrals

Gray Complementary Colors

Analogous with Gray Complements

Monochromatic Colors with Gray Complements

Analogous You can gray these colors, which are close to each other on the color wheel, by mixing their complements.

Monochromatic In a one-color scheme, such as blue, you would gray or darken the area by using its complement, in this case orange.

Split Complementary Achieve a split-complementary color scheme by choosing one color and using the two colors on each side of that color's complement on the color wheel. Use the complement of the middle color to gray the mixture.

Split Complements

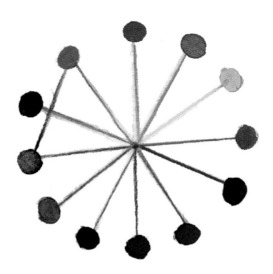

ARTIST'S TIP

When mixing colors, rinse your brush between each color to avoid contaminating the next color.

MIXING MUD

IT'S QUITE EASY for beginners to inadvertently create "mud" when mixing and applying color. Muddy colors, or colors that lack light, can be avoided if you initially stick to two-color mixtures and use transparent colors.

Mixing three primary colors together will create a muddy color unless the mixture is handled very carefully.

Mixing complementary opaque colors can result in mud even more frequently. The sediment in the mixture will prevent the white of the paper from shining through. To prevent this from happening when mixing grays from a complementary pair of colors, make sure that you allow one color to slightly dominate the mixture.

Mud also can result from layering or glazing one color over another. If you first lay down an opaque color and then glaze

Split Complements in Action

Before the Move
Marcia Moses, 22×30 inches

another color on top, the first layer will be disturbed and mix with the next layer, creating a dirty color. This is why it's important when layering or glazing to apply opaque colors last and to use staining colors as the under layers.

On the other hand, "mud" is a relative term and can be truly assessed only in relation to surrounding colors. Sometimes a muddy color may be exactly what is needed in a certain painting. In these cases, the artist has deliberately chosen to create a muddy color to achieve a specific effect or to set off other, brighter colors.

Time-Honored Techniques

PUTTING THEORY TO WORK

Now that we've learned about composition, design, color, values, and other important basics, we're ready to apply these theories to painting. Artists use a wide variety of techniques. Let's consider many techniques that both beginners and more accomplished artists can use effectively and successfully.

When beginners first apply paint to paper, they often feel frustrated when trying to create what they visualize. When I began painting, I often looked at paintings by experienced artists and wondered, "How did he get that sky to look so wonderful?" Or I would think, "That looks like a real tree. How did she do that?"

Of course, technique is the answer to those questions and to others that plague beginners. While there are countless painting styles, all use many basic watercolor techniques, such as washes and controlled drip, or even throwing, spattering, and pouring. Your painting may have a perfect design and a well-developed plan, but these won't be evident on paper without a working knowledge of the basic techniques necessary to achieve your artistic goal.

ARTIST'S TIP

If you combine too many special effects, your painting may appear chaotic.

Martha's Vineyard
Marcia Moses, 11 × 14 inches

BASIC WASHES

ARTISTS USE FOUR BASIC washes to cover large areas of paper. They are wet on wet, wet on dry, dry on wet, and dry on dry.

Wet on Wet

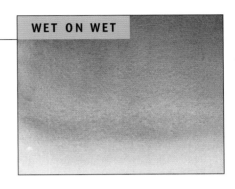

This wet-on-wet technique refers to applying wet paint on wet paint or applying wet paint on dampened paper. For wet colors to mix properly on the paper, the color and the water both need to be equally wet. If the water on the brush is too wet, the color will almost disappear on the paper. You can use this wet-on-wet technique to produce such effects as a sky with blended colors or water that appears mirrorlike.

Wet on Dry

With the wet-on-dry technique, the paper will absorb the wet paint and allow you to control where you put the paint. With this process you'll get hard edges.

The wet-on-dry technique works nicely for some parts of the painting, but you'll also want to use other methods of applying paint to create soft edges that will be more pleasing to the eye.

Dry on Wet

For the dry-on-wet technique, use moist paint on a damp brush with all excess water squeezed out and paint on wet paper. You will be able to achieve a diffusion that will push elements into the background. This is great for background foliage, stands of trees, or mountains seen in the distance.

Dry on Dry

For the dry-on-dry technique, load a brush with thick paint and brush over dry paper. You'll achieve the best effects on rough paper.

This technique is useful for creating definition and texture. I use the dry-on-dry method to apply texture to trees, rocks, weather-beaten boards, and other objects.

GRADATED WASHES

There are two types of gradated washes: **tonal** gradation and **color** gradation.

- **Tonal wash** gradates from dark to light by adding a small amount of water to the brush each time you make a stroke. It uses a single color of paint.
- **Color wash** gradates from one color to another.

For the tonal wash (on this page, below), I loaded my brush with vermilion and applied one stroke. Then I dipped my brush gently into the water and made another stroke. You can continue this procedure as far down the paper as you want the tonal wash to go.

TONAL WASH

For both color washes on page 51, I used cadmium yellow light and cobalt blue. After wetting the entire paper, you can apply a wash of cadmium yellow light to half of the paper. Turn the paper upside down and apply a wash of cobalt blue down into the edge of the yellow. Turn the paper to allow the colors to mix. Lay the paper flat when you get the results you want. This technique is often used to create spectacular sunsets.

These color washes (right and below) use the same two colors of paint, cadmium yellow light and cobalt blue, with rather different but equally appealing results.

COLOR WASH

COLOR WASH

NEGATIVE PAINTING

WATERCOLOR, A UNIQUE and challenging method of painting, has gotten a bad reputation for being a difficult medium to work in. Novices may have had this notion because they didn't take the time to learn proper watercolor techniques. On the other hand, a few experienced and vain artists who wanted others to imagine that what they did was extremely difficult may have added to watercolor's reputation. However, watercolor painting is no more difficult than any other artistic medium as long as you know how to use watercolor techniques to achieve your desired results. You can control your watercolors or you can let them control you.

It is true that watercolor may be more unforgiving because it's tougher to hide mistakes than in, say, oil painting. A successful watercolor does require planning.

Negative painting involves painting in areas surrounding objects to which you want to draw viewers' attention. It's one of the most important techniques you'll ever learn for controlling watercolors and requires a little patience and planning to use it to your advantage.

ARTIST'S TIP

If a wash does not hold, use less water.

Monhegan House, unfinished painting
Marcia Moses, 11 × 14 inches

Monhegan House, finished painting
Marcia Moses, 11 × 14 inches

When correctly used, however, the results of negative painting will satisfy you and appeal even to casual viewers of your work.

Consider the watercolor "Monhegan House" for an example in negative painting. Here are two versions. The first shows the unfinished painting (on p. 52) with light and dark next to each other below the house already added.

In the second version (above), I've painted trees behind the house in a darker color for contrast, and I've painted a darker shade of blue at the bottom of the painting to make the rocky area and the house come forward. This was also negative painting. I added dark hues, which enhanced the lighter areas of the watercolor. Dark areas recede, and light areas come forward.

Controlled Drip

In this painting of a tree, I used the controlled drip method to allow the paint to blend on the paper.

1. I began by drawing the tree, sketching only minor details, just enough to create the dominant shape. With a brush, I spread water on the places where I wanted the paint to flow.

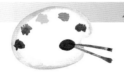

ARTIST'S TIP

To get paint to move on paper, spray it with water and tilt your board.

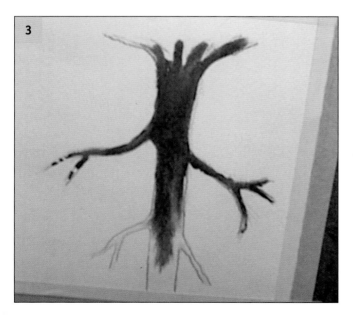

3. I could have applied the paint from the top of the tree and let the paint flow from the top, from dark to light, although this time I chose to do the opposite. I held the painting upside down and let paint flow from its bottom.

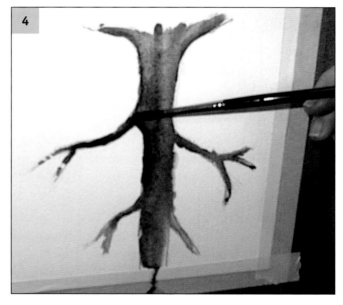

4. To force the paint to move and cover the paper, I pulled it with my brush.

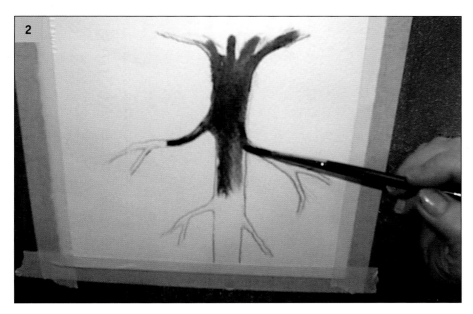

2. *Then I loaded the brush with a mixture of ultramarine blue and burnt sienna. I turned the paper upside down and began to apply the paint. I gently allowed the water to pull the paint from the brush. I was not actually brushing the paint; I was coaxing the paint to move. Tilting the board forced the paint to flow on the watered surface, but the paint stayed within the watered perimeters of the drawing.*

5. *After the tree was covered with paint, I used a crumpled tissue to lift paint in a pattern of lights and darks to give the tree three-dimensional form and create movement.*

Lilacs,
Marcia Moses, 22 × 30 inches

SPATTERING & THROWING PAINT

SOMETIMES I LOVE to throw paint on my white paper and then figure out where to go next. This exercise not only gets the juices flowing, but it can be a great way to let off steam.

There are a lot of different ways to throw or spatter paint. You can create large spatters with a very wet brush that's loaded with paint by flicking your wrist at the paper. Or create smaller spatters by tapping the end of the brush against the wrist of your other arm. For an even smaller spattering effect, draw your thumb over the bristles of a paint-laden brush pointed at a particular area of your paper.

In the painting "Lilacs" (above), I began without a plan and just threw paint on my paper. Mixing alizarin and royal blue makes a beautiful violet.

In the painting "Pots" (p. 57), I began by throwing and spattering three colors: ultramarine blue, aureolin yellow, and burnt sienna. I saw lots of textures begin to emerge, so I decided to play on that by adding many intertwining shapes.

Pots,
Marcia Moses, 18×24 inches

GLAZING

Glazing is a technique, using transparent paints, that maintains the paint's luminosity and allows lights to shine through. This happens when you apply a very thin layer of transparent paint to watercolor paper, allow it to dry, and apply the next layer of paint (whether of the same color or another color). For glazing, do not mix colors. Use only transparent colors to prevent mud.

Drying is the most important step in the glazing process. When you dry paint, it sets the color. That means that this color will not be disturbed by the next color you apply. The result is that the first color shines through the second and so on. I have used as many as fifty glazes in a single painting, and the colors keep shining through.

If the glaze (transparent paint layer) dries naturally, it will take a few minutes. If you use a hand held (blow) hair dryer, you can dry the glaze very quickly.

In the painting "Pots" (p. 57), I moved into the background to apply glazes beginning with aureolin. I added glazes of burnt sienna and ultramarine blue. After another drying, I began again with thin layers of each color. I dried between glazes to preserve their transparency.

Glazing allows you to apply many thin paint layers, and it helps prevent colors from becoming muddy. Keep in mind that you need to think out each layer you glaze. For example, if you glaze a layer of yellow, and then add a blue glaze, the color that results from the second layer will be green.

 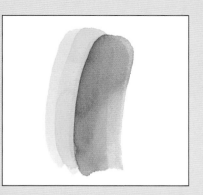

Glazing (Dry between glazes.)
cadmium yellow light +
rose madder + cobalt blue

Glazing (Dry between glazes.)
2 glazes of cadmium yellow light
+ 1 glaze of cobalt blue

LAYERING

IN WATERCOLOR, LAYERING uses much the same technique as glazing but with different results. That's because you do not dry between paint applications. Therefore, if you apply the first layer or wash of paint, then immediately apply the second and third layer without drying, the colors will mix on the paper, intertwining and creating magical effects. This technique of mixing wet on wet paint can fashion beautiful skies, wonderful sunsets, and numerous other exciting creations.

Practice with different transparent colors using only the three primary colors until you're comfortable using the layering technique. Avoid using opaque colors for layering, just as you would for glazing, to prevent mud.

Layering
Wet on wet: cadmium yellow light + rose madder + cobalt blue

CREATING TEXTURE

AFTER YOU'VE LEARNED watercolor basics, you can begin to add texture and dimension to your paintings. Many texture techniques are fun, and you'll be happy with the results.

When working on a painting that still hasn't come alive, consider whether it could be improved with texture. Texture can provide the illusion of three dimensions, raising a painting out of a flat two-dimensional surface and imbuing it with lifelike qualities.

In the watercolor "Stars and Stripes" (below), artist William Persa makes it possible to almost feel the texture of the soft, worn cloth flag against the old, battered wooden building. When I saw his painting, I wanted to capture what I saw and felt. The painting moved me with its incredible texture. And, I must confess, the composition drew on my patriotism and filled me with emotion.

Stars and Stripes
William Persa, 22×30 inches

Watercolor techniques like *spattering, spritzing, glazing, dry brushing, lifting off paint,* and *scraping* allow you to create just the right texture for rocks, trees, water, weathered wood, flowers, foliage, fences, and whatever else you may need. Artists often use the dry-on-dry technique, using a dry brush with more paint than water on dry paper, to add definition, depth, and appealing texture to their paintings.

For *lifting paint off* or out of paper, tools that work well include a wet brush, dry brush, sponge, facial tissue, paper towel, cotton swab, eraser, brush handle, or sandpaper. Most tools can work on wet paint. If you use sandpaper, first let the paint dry. You can also create texture by using a razor blade, putty knife, spatula, wax paper, stamp, alcohol, bleach, or even tap water.

For *scraping off paint,* common household tools, like a razor blade, putty knife, expired credit card, or small rubber spatula, do the trick. Be sure to use a safety handle with the razor blade.

These various texturing techniques help create definitive shapes —the illusion of depth, roughness, and smoothness. Most don't even require a paintbrush.

Brush handle on 140# Arches cold-pressed paper.

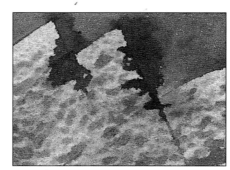

Old credit card on 140# rough paper.

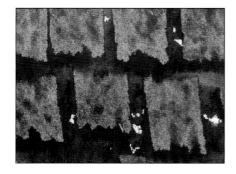

Small spatula on 140# Arches cold-pressed paper.

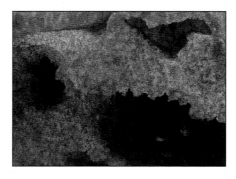

Large spatula on 140# rough paper.

Water Spritz

Use water in a spray bottle or atomizer to spritz on snow, flowers, or the spray of a wave. The water helps move paint around on the paper. Spritzing with water will spread the colors out and leave lighter spots or allow colors to mix.

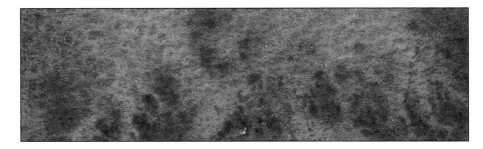

Spritz with water on 140# rough paper.

Salt

Salt sprinkled on wet paint absorbs color surrounding each salt crystal. After the paint dries, brush the salt from the paper to find the blossoms of light spots. Use various kinds of salt to create the desired texture. Table salt makes nice snowflakes, kosher or sea salt shapes flowers, and rock salt (used for melting ice outdoors) creates abstract, craterlike shapes. The larger the salt crystal, the more paint absorbed. Of course, the more salt you use, the more paint will be absorbed also. Ocean beach sand, which contains a lot of salt, also works nicely to remove paint from paper.

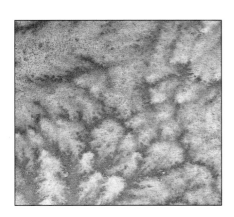

Table salt on wet paint with 140# rough paper.

Sea salt on 140# rough paper.

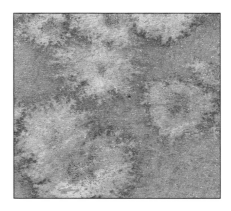

Rock salt on 140# rough paper.

Razor Blade

For this log, I applied wet paint into dry paint. First I used aureolin yellow and let it dry. Then I charged the brush with burnt sienna and a cobalt blue hue. I pushed the wet colors around with a razor blade, trying to create the log's characteristic ridges and bumps. I added a little detail with a #4 round brush.

Razor blade on 140# rough paper.

Sponge

Use a natural sponge dipped into paint to paint a stand of trees. Sap green mixed with a little rose madder over aureolin yellow created this group. To have a little more control, keep most of the sponge free of paint.

Brush Handle Tip

Here is a little exercise for painting grass that's gratifying for both beginners and professionals. Try these steps to create believable grass.

Painting Grass

1. *Apply a wash of sap green and charge your brush with a little aureolin yellow and a little rose madder.*

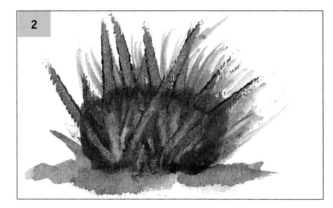

2. *Using the end of your fingernail or the flat end of a brush handle tip, scrape upward through the wash, beginning at the bottom, and pull the paint out and up above the wash.*

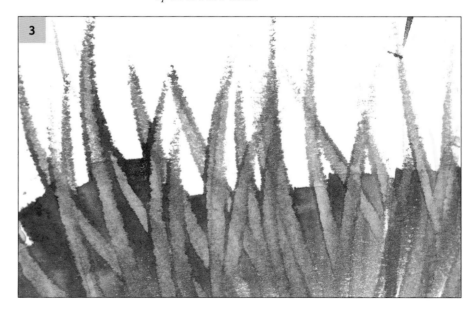

3. *The finished product shows how you can take a flat surface, paper, and create a three-dimensional object on it, grass. Use this technique to create texture on a variety of other objects you paint, including trees, rocks, and flower stems.*

Wax Paper

For this painting, I first used a wash of sap green over the watercolor paper's entire surface. Then I pressed wax paper down on the top half of the paper and allowed it to dry. After I removed the wax paper, I found this incredible texture that pushed my imagination to work overtime. Could this be a forest, waterfall, or lake? Dozens of things seemed possible.

Wax paper used to remove paint.

Plastic Wrap

If you apply plastic wrap to wet paint on rough paper, then remove it, you'll discover interesting textures.

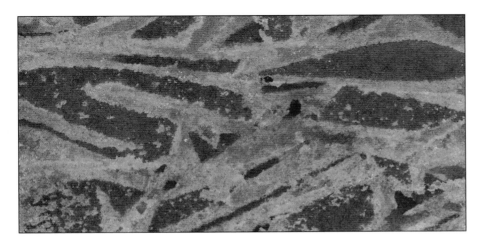

Plastic wrap on 140# rough paper.

Stamping

My earliest exercises in using a stamp felt like cheating. Don't worry; you'll have too much fun playing with great stamping tools to imagine that. Buy a few inexpensive rubber stamps from a craft store. Later you may want to make your own by cutting designs out of stiff illustration board with an X-acto knife.

For this forest of trees, I used my homemade stencil. I didn't feel a bit guilty that I didn't use a brush. Remember that there are many ways to create art. Feel free to use them to complete your painting. So, paint and stamp away. As long as you paint from your heart, there's no wrong way to create your finished work.

Stamping

Alcohol

Alcohol is the perfect substance for creating texture. With watercolor paint, alcohol can help move the paint and spread it into all kinds of shapes. Alcohol may also be used to remove or lift paint.

To create the bark's texture, I painted wet on wet paint. First I applied cobalt blue; then I charged burnt sienna into the wash and allowed it to mix on paper. Finally, I used a spray bottle containing alcohol, carefully spraying little shots into the paint to give the tree trunk and branches the look I wanted.

Alcohol for creating texture and removing paint.

ARTIST'S TIP

When lifting off color, use a clean facial tissue to prevent accidental mixing of colors.

POURING COLOR

Pouring color can create wonderfully luminous effects. You can get an effect that cannot be accomplished by merely stroking the brush on paper. It allows you to create movement, mood, and texture. The technique can be a bit unpredictable, but that's part of its charm.

Choosing Paper

My favorite paper is Strathmore Imperial cold-pressed 500 series 140-pound paper. It does not hold poured paint as well as the other brands, but I like the results. Arches 140-pound cold-pressed paper is more porous and takes pouring well, as it absorbs paint more quickly. Strathmore Imperial tends to take on a light coat of paint, so I usually pour onto this paper twice to achieve the desired luminosity. Strathmore Imperial is more forgiving than many other kinds of paper. To get back the paper's white, simply use a damp brush and lightly wash out the color. This technique doesn't necessarily work on other watercolor paper.

Stretching Paper

Before you begin pouring paint, soak the watercolor paper to remove some of its sizing (a material used to make the paper surface less absorbent). I usually soak my paper in the bathtub for about 10 minutes. Then I remove it and staple it to a gator board or any other hard, durable surface to dry.

I've also had good experience with unprepared paper, although I highly recommend using stretched paper.

Preserving Whites

Masking fluid does the trick to preserve white areas you want to use. (I prefer Incredible White Mask liquid frisket.) First use a soap without additives (such as Ivory hand soap) to wet and lather an old brush. Dip the lathered brush into the mask. With each new stroke, repeat this action.

Allow the mask to dry completely before you paint over it. The mask may take several hours to dry. After pouring or painting, you can remove the mask with a gum eraser and continue to paint. You can also apply the mask over paint to preserve certain areas or colors in preparation for a new pouring.

Golden Gate,
Marcia Moses, 22 × 30 inches

Mixing Color

To mix color for pouring, use a bottle, dish, cup, or another container. I've tried paper cups, ketchup bottles, plates, bowls, and many other household items.

Depending on the intensity you want, mix a strong color (four parts water to one part paint) or weak colors (eight parts water to one part paint). Check the properties of each paint so that you will know what patches of color you'll be able to remove or lift out.

Pouring without a Plan

Prepare the paper and allow it to dry. Re-wet it with a simple water wash and poured color, allowing the color to mix on the paper by moving the board around until the mix pleases you. After this mix has dried, consider the shapes you see. Decide what the composition could say. Pull out shapes with a brush and water. If you use easy-lift paint, it will be a cinch to create these shapes.

Pouring with a Plan

When pouring with a plan, you'll want to think about each step before you begin work. Ask yourself:

- What is your **design,** and what kind of shape do you want it to take?
- Where do you want to **preserve** whites?
- How **intense** do you want the colors, and what do you want them to say?
- Are your colors **transparent** and easy to lift from the paper (if you want to control them a bit or avoid "mistakes")?

Painting Step-by-Step

Leaves

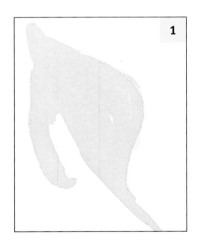

1. *With a #4 round brush, wet the entire area of the leaf with water. Apply a wash of aureolin yellow on the shape.*

2. *Immediately charge the wash with ultramarine blue, allowing colors to mix. With tissue or cotton swab, lift off color to reveal a little white shape for light. Let dry. With a wet brush, glaze this with a wash of aureolin yellow.*

3. *Apply a wash of ultramarine blue on the dark side of the leaf, maintaining the lights previously lifted with the tissue on the opposite side. Finish the leaf by pulling out veins with a damp brush and tissue.*

Watermelon

In most of my paintings, I use a basic palette that consists of aureolin yellow, rose madder, and cobalt blue hues. This represents the three primary colors. However, depending on the painting's needs, sometimes I develop another palette with colors that better suit my subject.

For watermelons, I wanted a palette that would give me a little more flexibility, so I chose cadmium yellow light, rose madder, and marine blue.

1. *Using a 1-inch flat brush, I painted a wash of cadmium yellow light on the entire shape of a half watermelon.*

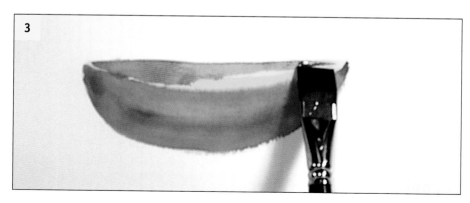

2. *I charged this wash with marine blue, and this gave me the green I wanted for the watermelon shell.*

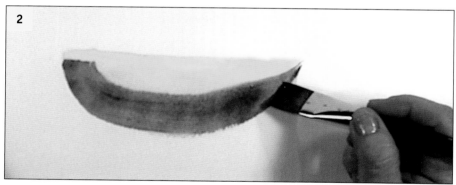

3. *With rose madder, I painted a light wash inside the watermelon that began to draw out the pink of the fruit.*

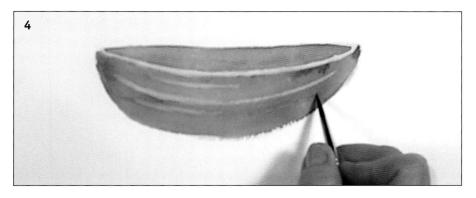

4. *With marine blue, I put some darks in the shell's bottom right part to create a shadow. Then I blended this with my brush and water.*

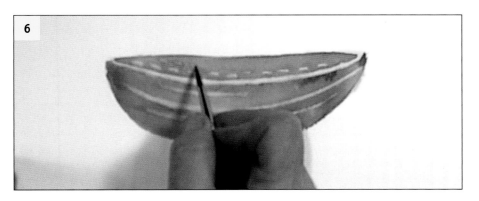

5. *With a tissue I pulled off a little rose madder and yellow to produce lights inside the watermelon.*

6. *I used a brush dipped in water to pull out the remaining watermelon seeds.*

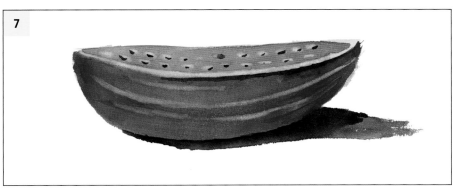

7. *With a mixture of cadmium yellow light, rose madder, and a drop of marine blue, I began final detailing. I used this color mixture for the seeds, the shadow on the surface under the watermelon, and the dark shell shapes.*

Rocks

It's great fun to paint rocks. What results from this exercise is always a surprise. And while you may not like surprises, when painting rocks you'll be able to feel your creative spirit come alive. This kind of surprise is delightful compared to, say, a houseguest who arrives without warning and plans to stay three weeks.

Ready? Get out your ½-inch flat brush, an old expired credit card or plastic putty knife, salt, alcohol, perfume (you'll be able to smell the texture), facial tissue, burnt sienna, indigo, ultramarine dark, water, and last but not least, a toothbrush. (Yes, use the one your unexpected houseguest left.) Let's get started!

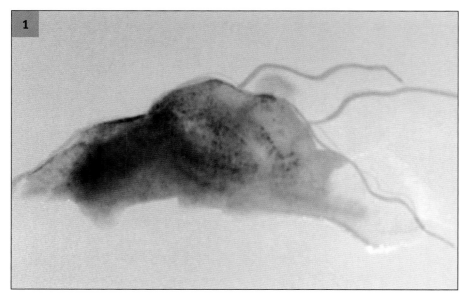

1. *Lightly sketch rock formations on your watercolor paper. I recommend Fabriano-Rosaspina or Strathmore Imperial; these papers do not have a heavy texture. They will allow you to create your own texture.*
  Wet the positive areas and leave a dry white separation between the shapes.
  Begin to drop color and let it flow in all directions. It doesn't matter which color you drop first.

2. *Let the colors mix on the paper, and while they're still wet, use your credit card or plastic putty knife to move color around, creating shapes.*

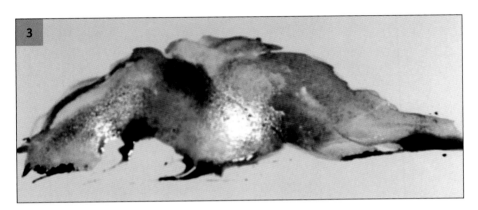

3. *With each introduction of color, you'll discover a new effect. Because ultramarine is a sedimentary color, it will create texture when mixed on paper with burnt sienna. When moving colors, make sure you place lights next to darks for the illusion of motion and drama. While the paint is still wet, spray alcohol or perfume on it and watch what happens. Sprinkle salt on spots where you want to lift paint and create texture. Paint darks in shadowed areas. Spatter both colors with a toothbrush to add more texture. Experiment with these tools, and by all means, have fun. With a crumpled tissue, lift areas you want to lighten and watch what happens.*

FINISHED PAINTING

4. *Lay a small sheet of plastic wrap on areas where you may want more texture. The plastic wrap will create small lines of texture.*

Magnolias

To reproduce this magnolia, I studied the flower and came to know its many beautiful shapes, colors, and values. It's much easier to paint what you know than to rush blindly into a painting without studying the subject.

1. First, I sketched the magnolia in my sketchbook using only three values. This preliminary sketch helped me decide where colors and shadow would be needed. Then on watercolor paper, with my pencil, I reproduced the bigger shapes from that initial sketch.

2. Before I began painting, I decided where color values would be darkest and lightest. Using an initial glaze of aureolin yellow, I began to paint, carefully painting around the flower shapes to preserve the whites.

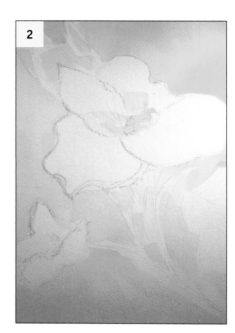

3. The initial glaze with aureolin yellow established the background for the larger shapes.

4. Next I introduced marine blue, a blue-green transparent color that allows the yellow glaze to show through. Marine blue is a blue with a long value range from a mild green-blue to a rich, vibrant, deep blue-green. I began with a watered-down light value of this color and glazed areas around the largest shape.

5. *I continued to glaze a second layer of the marine blue around the larger shapes, which made my blues darker. With light and dark colors next to each other, my flower began to appear three-dimensional. Then I waited for the glazes to dry.*

Next I glazed a layer of aureolin yellow around larger shapes and waited for them to dry. Then I applied a layer of marine blue. This time, however, I didn't dry them because I wanted to mix a little of the wet paint with another color on the paper. This would give the background a little texture.

6. *With the marine blue, mixed with very little water, I began to paint details, such as the flower's center, the spaces between stems, and the flower's shadows.*

Then I took the marine blue in mid-value, and glazed the bottom left and top middle. While that was still wet, I glazed the bottom right and top left with aureolin. I let them dry.

At this point, I began pulling off paint with a damp brush. I clarified whites on the stem, pulled whites out of the leaves, and finished by adding details with burnt sienna on the darker side of the magnolia's stems and stamens.

Glazed Bottles

1. *After sketching the bottles, I applied thin coats of paint around the objects, creating a background. I began with aureolin yellow and allowed this to dry so that my next glaze would not pick up the aureolin.*

2. *Next I applied a glaze of alizarin crimson. Keep in mind that if you want to preserve any lights, you need to do it in these early stages. I wanted the top right area to be lighter, so I didn't glaze over it.*

3. *Notice the darker paint colors in the left half of the background. If paint is too wet, it will gather in pockets. If you want to create a textured background, this could work to your advantage.*

  I didn't, so I merely collected that darker paint with the edge of a tissue.

4. *To tone things down, I added another transparent color—a glaze of ultramarine dark. I needed to be careful not to add too much blue to the already orange tone, which would cause a muddy or dull appearance. By applying only a thin glaze of blue, I also preserved the painting's luminosity.*

While adding the blue glaze, I decided to bring a little blue into my objects. I pulled the brush inside the bottle outlines.

5. *I began adding details to objects between glazes. Sometimes I try to work in another area of a painting while the glaze dries naturally. Blow-drying the glaze sometimes moves the paint in an undesirable way.*

After glazing numerous times, alternating with the three primary colors to create a unified effect, I did a little spattering to create texture on the bottles. I used a toothbrush, dipping the bristles into ultramarine blue and using my thumb on the brush to spatter the color lightly.

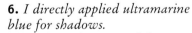

6. *I directly applied ultramarine blue for shadows.*

In the end, I wanted the painting to look old and the bottles to look as though they had been sitting in a wine cellar for decades. For aging, I used a blue glaze over all but my lights. This softened bottle edges and shadows and gave the painting a more subtle appearance.

After a little more detailing, such as lifting paint off the lights in the grapes in the foreground, I was finished.

Painting Step-by-Step   **79**

INDEX